inch by inch

KOBAYASHI ISSA

inch by inch

45 HAIKU BY ISSA

translated by Nanao Sakaki

La Alameda Press   Albuquerque

La Alameda Press
9636 Guadalupe Trail NW
Albuquerque, New Mexico 87114

Contents

Translator's Note

Kobayashi Issa (1763-1827) was born in Kashiwabara village, Shinano, Japan. His family members were middle class farmers and serious Buddhists of the Pure Land Sect. Most of the time he lived in Edo (old-time Tokyo), occasionally traveling as a vagabond poet, he lived a rather sad life.

Not gifted with genius, but honestly holding his experience deep in his heart, he kept his simplicity and humanity.

Very skeptical of authorities, either political or religious, he (after Bashō's revolutionary breakthrough) opened the democratic trail for common people.

Once on a rainy day, I visited Kashiwabara, where Issa died. There, with his family, he lies under a humble tombstone.

Nanao Sakaki

初螢 なぜ引きかえす おれだぞよ

First lightning bug this year
Why do you turn away?
It's me, Issa!

Hatsubotaru Naze Hikikaesu Oredazoyo

浮草の　花から乗らん　あの雲へ

Let's ride
on the duckweed flowers
to a cloud over there

Ukigusano Hanakaranoran Anokumoe

鳴きながら　虫の流るる　浮木かな

Singing high —
A cricket on a log
floating down the river

Nakinagara Mushinonagaruru Ukigikana

小便の たらたら下や 杜つばた

Pissing pissing
Down there
    an iris blooming

Shobenno Tara-tarashitaya Kakitsubata

かたつむり そろそろ登れ富士の山

Inch by inch —
Little snail
Creep up and up Mt. Fuji

Katatsumuri Soro-soronobore Fujinoyama

そよ風は　蝉の声より　起るかな

It begins
from the cicada's song
The gentle breeze

Soyokazewa Seminokoeyori Okorukana

大井川見えて　それから雲雀かな

Here, the River Oi
And after that
　　— a skylark

Ōigawa Mieta Sorekara Hibarikana

うぐいすや どろ足ぬぐう 梅の花

Upon the blooming plum twig
a warbler
wipes his muddy feet

Uguisuya Doroashinuguu Umenohana

追ろな 追ろな 追ろな子供よ 子持のみ

Children, don't!
Don't catch the flea!
She, too, has children

Ōuna Ōuna Ōuna Kodomoyo Komochinomi

我が袖を　草と思うか　違うほたる

A firefly
creeping up my sleeve
OK,　I'm a blade of grass

Wagosodeo Kusatoomouka Hau Hotaru

やせ蛙 負けるな 一茶ここにあり

Don't give up the game
skinny frog!
Issa is here

Yaegaeru Makeruna Issa Kokoniari

花のかげ 赤の他人は なかりけり

Who can be
a stranger
under the cherry blossoms?

Hananokage Akanotaninwa Nakarikeri

苔清水 さあ 鳩もこよ 雀こよ

From mossy stones
clear water — ha!
Come on pigeons, sparrows!

Kokeshimizu Sa Hatomokoyo Suzumekoyo

菊咲くや 馬ぐそ山も ひとけしき

what a picture —
By the pile of horse dung
Chrysanthemums in full bloom

Kikusakuya Magusoyamamo Hitokeshiki

我ときて 遊べや 親のない雀

Come play with me!
you, little sparrow
    motherless sparrow!

Waretokite Asobeya Oyanonai Suzume

27

蟻の道　雲の峯よりつづきけん

The ant's trail
From a thunderhead
  all the way to here!

Arinomichi Kumonomineyori Tsuzukiken

むぐらから　あんな胡蝶の生れけり

Such a beauty —
From the milkweed
　　a butterfly is born

Mugurakara Annakochōno Umarekeri

でで虫の その身 そのまま 寝起さかな

Just as he is
he goes to bed and gets up
         The snail —

Dedemushino Sonomi Somomama Neokikana

やぶ影や たった一人の 田植うた

Alone in a shady paddy
one woman sings
a rice-planting song

Yabukageya Tattahitorino Taueuta

31

大根びき 大根で道おしえけり

The daikon picker
points the way
              with his daikon

Daikonbiki Daikonde Michi Oshiekeri

でで出や 赤い花には眼もかけず

Not even a glance
at the scarlet flower —
A snail creeping

Dedemushiya Akaihananiwa Memokakezu

かたつむり 見よ 見よ おのが 影法師

Snail!
Look — look
　　at your own shadow!

Katatsumuri Miyo Miyo Onogakageboshi

人あれば 蠅あり 佛ありにけり

Without human beings
no fly
no Buddha

Hitoareba Haeari Hotokearinikeri

ごちゃごちゃと やせ蚊 やせ蚤 やせ子かな

Thin mosquitoes, thin fleas
thin children ―all mixed up
here in my house

Gocha Gochato Yaseka Yasenomi Yasegokana

美しさや　障子の穴の　天の川

How lovely
through the torn paper window
— the Milky Way

Utsukushisaya Shōjinoanano Amenokawa

むだ草や　汝も伸べる　日ものべる

The sun, getting higher
Summer weeds
　　　you, too, are higher

Mudagusaya Nanjimonobiru Himonobiru

長生きの 蝿や蚤 蚊や貧乏村

Flies, fleas, mosquitoes
and people — all long lived
in my poor village

Nagaikino Haeya Nomikaya Binbōmura

寝た人を　畫飯喰いにきた　蚊かな

O mosquitoes!
You have lunch
on a man taking a nap

Netahitoo Hirumeshi Kuinikita Kakana

人を取る 茸 はたして美しき

The Amanita muscaria
can kill you —
sure, what a beauty!

Hitootoru Kinoko Hatashite Utsukushiki

がさがさと ちまきをかじる 美人かな

A beautiful girl
munching, munching
a rice - dumpling

Gasa Gasato Chimakiokajiru Bijinkana

雀の子 そこのけ そこのけ お馬がとおる

Get out, little sparrow!
Get out of the way!
Mr. Horse is coming

Suzumenoko Sokonoke Soconoke Oumagatooru

43

やれ打つな 蝿が 手をする 足をする

Don't swat the fly
who begs your pardon
wringing his hands and legs

Yare Utsuna Haega Teosuru Ashiosuru

44

前の世の おれがいとこか 閑古どり

Hi cuckoo!
wasn't I your cousin
in another life?

Maenoyono Oregaitokoka Kankodori

けろりくわんとして からすと やなぎかな

As if nothing-had happened
— the crow there
the willow here

Kerori Kuwantoshite Karasuto Yanagikana

人ひとり　蠅ひとつや　大屋敷

Just myself
Also, one fly
— an enormous house

Hitohitori Haehitotsuya Ōyashiki

ふたつ居て　ひとつは鳴かず　秋の蝉

One sings
The other will sing no more
— cicadas of Autumn

Futatsuite Hitotsuwa Nakazu Akinosemi

陽の蜘蛛 巣じな すすはとらぬぞよ

Spiders in the corner
Don't worry!
I won't sweep your house

Suminokumo Anjina Susuwa Tranuzoyo

蚤どもも 夜ながだろうぞ 淋しかろ

Long autumn night —
Fleas
you, too, must be lonesome

Nomidomomo Yonagadarozo Sabishikaro

一本の草も　すず風　やどりけり

On a single blade of grass
a cool breeze
lingers

Ipponnokusamo Suzukaze Yadorikeri

遠山が　眼玉にうつる　とんぼかな

The distant mountains
in your eyes
　　　Mr. Dragonfly

Tōyamaga Medamaniutsuru Tommbokana

能なしは　罪も又なし　冬ごもり

No talent
No blame, either
Now I'm in winter retreat

Nōnashiwa Tsumimomatanashi Fuyugomori

うまそうな雪が ふうはり ふうはりと

The snow wafting —
wafting — down
Down   — I could eat it!

Umasōna Ukiga Fūwari Fūwarito

54

我死なば 墓守りになれと きりぎりす

Grasshopper, good singer!
Take care of my tomb
when I die

Wareshinaba Hakamorininareto Kirigirisu

55

長いぞよ 夜が長いぞよ なむあみだ

Long—
So long is the night
— Namu Amida

Nagaizoyo Yoganagaizoyo Namu Amida

ただ居れば居るとて雪の降りにけり

Simply, I'm here
Simply, snow falls

Tadaoreba Orutote Yukinofurinikeri

Cup of Tea, Plate of Fish
an interview with Nanao Sakaki

This conversation with John Brandi and Jeff Bryan took place in
the middle Rio Grande watershed, Corrales, New Mexico, under
old mulberry and cottonwood trees, amidst bird call and cricket
chirp, between bites of grilled tuna, miso-soup, and stout ale.

Brandi: Who first introduced you to Issa? How old were you?

Sakaki: Probably I was 8- or 9-year old boy, Japanese kids like
his haiku.

Bryan: Was this an awakening for you—a sense of AH, here's
someone I like?

Sakaki: Yeah—"Oh wow. Let's go!"

Brandi: Did reading Issa or knowing about his life, wandering
in Japan, influence you, make you want to write
poetry, wander and travel?

Sakaki: No, no, too late for me. I'd already started! I bought
this book about Issa in 1943, can you imagine?
Already the war had started. I was just 20 years old.

I carried this book into the Japanese navy. But not only Issa, I was reading Bashō and same time I was reading Shakespeare and same time Kropotkin. *(laughs)* A good combination!

Bryan: Was reading Issa and Bashō something accepted in the navy?

Sakaki: Sure, no trouble—but Kropotkin was real trouble.

Bryan: Did they know who he was?

Sakaki: No, they didn't really know anything about Kropotkin. I must tell them that he's sort-of-like Nazi, so it's OK. Shakespeare I explained to my upper officer . . . this is Kabuki, English kabuki . . . so it's OK.

Brandi: What about the differences between Issa and Bashō? How is Issa different?

Sakaki: I feel Bashō is more revolutionary personality. He was born upper class samurai, very good education, maybe too good of education. If he had no education, maybe he could have been much greater poet.

Brandi: And Issa's education?

Sakaki: Issa's more peasant, good for peasant. Like middle
           class because he's landowner . . . only a very small
           patch, still he was landowner, so landowner means
           middle class. Bashō mostly intellectual background.
           Issa nothing, no education, he learned only from his
           life. So that is more closer to everybody.

Bryan: Didn't Issa have a period where he lived on the streets
           after being driven from his family land by his step-
           mother?

Sakaki: Oh yeah, kind of hanging around anywhere.

Brandi: In Edo?

Sakaki: Yeah, a couple of times.

Bryan: Getting his street smarts?

Sakaki: Perhaps, sometimes I feel Bashō has no reality, Issa
           more reality.

Brandi: How did Issa, compared with a more modern poet
            like Santoka, open up a democratic road?

Sakaki: I'm not interested in Santoka.

Brandi: Why?

Sakaki: Sentimental, just sentimental, just himself, no society,
            no universe. He has no compassion for other animals,
            other beings. —See? . . . Just sentimental. But we need a
            sentimental poet too. *(laughs)* We need many poets!
            All kinds of poets!

Bryan: Issa had compassion?

Sakaki: Issa more compassionate, yes.

Brandi: Does Issa's compassion come from being born in the
            Buddhist Pure Land sect?

Sakaki: I don't think so.

Brandi: Where does it come from then?

Sakaki: It's human nature. It's human nature. All religion,
              all kinds of organization, or some kind of a guru
              wants us to think it's something we make. It's not
              true, everybody has it originated in our blood.

Brandi: Did Issa's background being a farmer's son affect
              his poetry?

Sakaki: A little bit, but not everything. We think we are the
              slave of experience, but not so, we are more free!
              Yeah, we can be more separated from our own experi-
              ence. Most people think experience, experience, but
              it's not true! We can jump over experience!

Bryan: Issa could leave behind his early family strife and just
              be himself.

Sakaki: Yes, most writers in Japan talk about this experience
              leading to this or that haiku— "If you come from poor
              society, then you think this way." What!? I don't
              think so, no need of such stuff. We have bigger riches,
              the world we live in. Issa's not a slave of his experi-
              ence, his life is something else.

Bryan: What is that something else?

Sakaki: Something else is more interesting stuff. Like . . . "What's that!?" *(smiling)*

Bryan: Issa saw the world differently—a sense of identification with things . . . with birds and bugs?

Sakaki: Yeah, true, true, they're him, it's not so far.

Bryan: They're right there.

Sakaki: My neighbor!

Brandi: In Japan is he more of a folk hero or a poet? Do many people like him because he was an old man, he had a hard life, he suffered, he wrote poetry?

Sakaki: No, maybe the other way . . . his poems are still alive. Everybody talking his haiku—still his haiku are alive, see? Life is second, I read so many books about him but after a point I say, "No, no get away from here! It's nonsense!"

Brandi: Because you want to read his poems?

Sakaki: Yes, his poems are most important, not his life! Georgia O'Keeffe said the same thing, she did, she wrote . . . my circumstances don't matter—but what I painted, that's important.

Brandi: When did you first start your walkings?

Sakaki: Oh, always the same question! My answer is—before I was born! *(laughter all around)*

Brandi: You mean you didn't start walking because you read Issa? *(laughs)*

Sakaki: No! Same question as "When did you start writing poetry?" I feel same way. OK, before I was born, I started writing poetry. HA! That's a true story. I wrote poetry many many centuries ago. Then they called me Bashō or Issa or Buson or Shakespeare.

Bryan: What is this spirit which carries on?

Sakaki:	I never think such a thought. Just I'm here, so I write something—and this is the echo of the ancients.
Brandi:	When we hiked up into the fossil range of the Sandias a few days ago, you opened your arms and said: "Everyday's tomorrow!" What does that mean?
Sakaki:	Yes, yes. Everyday's tomorrow. Maybe tomorrow I do this way, I go this way or that way. Every day we think: tomorrow tomorrow, so tomorrow is everyday. Everyday's a tomorrow. *(laughs)* It's very simple. Jesus Christ's time or Shakespeare's time or Chaplin's time, always tomorrow . . . always is tomorrow, never changing, yeah, always there, tomorrow, or next century, you can call it any name, next week, next year, or next life.
Brandi:	You mean next life, next century, is the same time as today?
Sakaki:	Yes. Nothing changes. *(laughs)* Congratulations! We walk the same way.
Bryan:	What's important about Issa's poems for us today? Do the poems have a special appeal?

Sakaki: OK, OK, probably in this time we need mostly a kind
            of happy, lucky feeling. We're completely losing this,
            everybody's so serious-faced, tight-faced, we really need
            humor, laughing, smiling, joking, such a feeling. That
            is something Issa had.

Bryan: Let's look at this poem, the poem where he
            announces his new name—

                    Haru tatsuya yataro aratame Issabo

Sakaki: This is just personal stuff; it's not so interesting.

Brandi: What is your translation of the poem?

Sakaki: I never translated this one, it has no meaning to me,
            too personal, too himself.

Bryan: So...many of Issa's poems you don't respond to?

Sakaki: No, 20,000 haiku he wrote—maybe 500 I can read.
            Maybe 200 I love. Maybe 10 great. Great stuff. It's a
            hard job, selecting his haiku. Many times I still check

his haiku, I still carry them around with me. Most of them so dull. But he was crazy about writing haiku!

Brandi: One of your translations in this book is:

>*just as he is*
>*he goes to bed and gets up*
>*the snail*

Did the snail show Issa how simple life can be in the middle of all our complications and things we need?

Sakaki: I guess so. That's a good understanding, yeah. But maybe something a little more wider. He feels jealousy, ah yeah *(laughs)* "I must think about money and human relations but the snail doesn't care, just goes to sleep, just walk around, eat . . . uh-oh, But not me, why? *Why*?" That is his point. Why is important, why is snail that way, why I'm this way . . . strange! *Why?* Why we are here, why is the sky so shiny, why trees so green?

Bryan: It's all so beautiful, why am I so uptight?

Sakaki: Yeah, the surprisement, that is haiku.

Bryan: We laugh, but at the same time we *get* something.

Sakaki: Yes, something comes suddenly—wisdom! *(laughs)*

Brandi: What about your translation of my very favorite of
              Issa's poems, it's not in **Inch by Inch**, but we've
              talked about it before.

              Tsuyu no wa tsuya no yo nagara sari nagara

Sakaki: OK, yeah. That's a hard one! So he had many
              children, all gone, so he felt this life is just dew, so
              temporary, so short life. Even though, I'm here. So,
              that's sad. "Why my daughter or my baby must die?
              What's the reason?"

Brandi: One time you said that the translation was:

              the world of dew
              is just the world of dew
              and yet . . . and yet

Sakaki: ". . . and yet." That is the point.

Brandi:	So he says I know the world of dew is just the world of dew, yet I feel pain, I am alive.
Sakaki:	So simple, simple, yet so wide.
Brandi:	What do you think happens when we die?
Sakaki:	I don't care.
Brandi:	Where is your friend Allen Ginsberg?
Sakaki:	Allen's somewhere, somewhere in space. I don't care. He's OK. He never talks to me, no complaining, nothing. It's OK.
Bryan:	We worry too much?
Sakaki:	We end up hanging around somewhere *(laughs)* or maybe changing to fish . . . yeah.
Brandi:	Like Issa, are you immortal because of what you've written, always there for other human beings?

Sakaki: Sure. We live in the same language, but maybe a little different way of expression. Each poet or writer or artist or musician is handing down most beautiful part of our culture . . . it's a gift.

Brandi: Are you part of Issa's lineage?

Sakaki: I think so. Not only Issa, but many other people, like Lao Tzu in China. Many beings come to me, from me, many rivers going down, running down—sure.

(wiggles his fingers like little streams coming off little streams)

Brandi: Running out from you?

Sakaki: Yeah—sure, kind of a river. Exactly.

(smiles, nods, everybody laughs)

COLOPHON

Set in *ITC Esprit*
by contemporary designer
& calligrapher Jovica Veljović.
Lively, flaired serifs impart
a brushy humor to a classic
structure giving the reader a
melodic off-kilter pleasure.

•

Book design by J. Bryan

Nanao Sakaki

When asked "How is it you feel better as you get older?"
Nanao, seventy-five years old, gave a clear response. "When
you are young you are too busy escaping, you are holding
yourself too tightly. When you are old, you see more deeply,
feel more deeply. So you are lighter. You have time.
Everything talks to you, everything is alive."